Light Universal Journal

Masami Light

Amesian Books

Welcome

Your wish is the Universe wish
Your wish is the Earth's wish
Your wish is a Future promise
to lead you
to the Universe and Earth's Future!

All Miracles of the Universe
start with your wish

あなたの願いは、宇宙ユニバースの願い
あなたの願いは、地球の願い
あなたの願いは、未来への約束
あなたを地球と宇宙の未来へ導き繋いでください！

宇宙のミラクルは全てあなたの願いから始まります

This belongs to

Your name あなたの名前

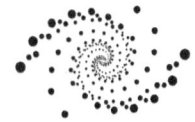

Trust the Universe Light
Trust Myself
to Create My Own Future
Promise to Love My Life

宇宙ユニバースの光とともに

自分自身を信じ

自分の未来を創り出します

自分の人生を愛することを約束します

Light Universe Signature 光の署名と共に

Love & Light

dreams come true

Love & Light

Love & Light

dreams come true

Love & Light

Love & Light

dreams come true

Love & Light

Love & Light

dreams come true

Love & Light

Love & Light

dreams come true

Love & Light

Love & Light

dreams come true

Love & Light

Love & Light

dreams come true

Love & Light

Love & Light

....
....
....
....
....
....
....
....
....
....
....
....
....
....
....
....
....
....
....
....
....
....

dreams come true

Love & Light

Love & Light

dreams come true

Love & Light

Love & Light

dreams come true

Love & Light

Love & Light

dreams come true

Love & Light

Love & Light

dreams come true

Love & Light

Love & Light

dreams come true

Love & Light

Love & Light

dreams come true

Love & Light

Love & Light

dreams come true

Love & Light

Love & Light

dreams come true

Love & Light

Love & Light

dreams come true

Love & Light

Love & Light

dreams come true

Love & Light

Love & Light

....
....
....
....
....
....
....
....
....
....
....
....
....
....
....
....
....
....
....
....
....
....
....

dreams come true

Love & Light

Love & Light

....
....
....
....
....
....
....
....
....
....
....
....
....
....
....
....
....
....
....
....
....
....
....

dreams come true

Love & Light

Love & Light

dreams come true

Love & Light

Love & Light

....
....
....
....
....
....
....
....
....
....
....
....
....
....
....
....
....
....
....
....
....
....

dreams come true

Love & Light

Love & Light

dreams come true

Love & Light

Love & Light

dreams come true

Love & Light

Love & Light

dreams come true

Love & Light

Love & Light

dreams come true

Love & Light

Love & Light

dreams come true

Love & Light

Love & Light

dreams come true

Love & Light

Love & Light

dreams come true

Love & Light

Love & Light

dreams come true

Love & Light

Love & Light

dreams come true

Love & Light

Love & Light

....
....
....
....
....
....
....
....
....
....
....
....
....
....
....
....
....
....
....
....
....
....
....
....

dreams come true

Love & Light

Love & Light

dreams come true

Love & Light

Love & Light

dreams come true

Love & Light

Love & Light

dreams come true

Love & Light

Love & Light

dreams come true

Love & Light

Love & Light

....
....
....
....
....
....
....
....
....
....
....
....
....
....
....
....
....
....
....
....
....
....

dreams come true

Love & Light

Love & Light

....
....
....
....
....
....
....
....
....
....
....
....
....
....
....
....
....
....
....
....
....
....
....

dreams come true

Love & Light

Love & Light

dreams come true

Love & Light

Love & Light

dreams come true

Love & Light

Love & Light

dreams come true

Love & Light

Love & Light

dreams come true

Love & Light

Love & Light

dreams come true

Love & Light

Love & Light

dreams come true

Love & Light

Love & Light

dreams come true

Love & Light

Love & Light

dreams come true

Love & Light

Love & Light

dreams come true

Love & Light

Love & Light

dreams come true

Love & Light

Love & Light

dreams come true

Love & Light

Love & Light

dreams come true

Love & Light

Love & Light

dreams come true

Love & Light

Love & Light

dreams come true

Love & Light

Love & Light

dreams come true

Love & Light

Love & Light

dreams come true

Love & Light

Love & Light

....
....
....
....
....
....
....
....
....
....
....
....
....
....
....
....
....
....
....
....
....
....

dreams come true

Love & Light

Love & Light

dreams come true

Congratulations

Are you ready for the next chapter?

あなたの創り出す

次なる世界への準備はできましたか？

著者

Masami Light

ライフスタイルプロモーター
イントゥイション（直観）スピーカー

マサミ ライト（本名）。沖縄県出身、ロサンゼルス在住。
高いエネルギーが溢れるヴォルテックスの土地に住む。自分と
家族が幸せで初めて人を助けることができると信じ、ライト
フィロソフィー発祥者として伝え続ける。代々高次力家系に生
まれ、幼少時より小人や妖精、宇宙人と様々な存在たちを引き
寄せる。20歳頃より相談するとビジネスが成功すると評判に。
大手企業のトップ達をはじめ多数の方が沖縄を訪れ、ビジネス
コンサルタントトークをするように。グローバルイベント相
談、億単位の交渉通訳など海外でも活躍の生活からLA移住後、
ライフビジョンプロモーターとしてSNS、ブログを通し発信。
家族中心の自由なライフスタイルを楽しむ。
大好きなのは主婦＆母親業。

Life Work & Gift Work　～適職 & 天職～

観音様が枕元に立ちメッセージを送ったことから某MLM企業
に携わる。カリスマ成功者のプライベート通訳をはじめ、100
名を超えるビジネス界のミリオネアたちの通訳としても活躍。
通訳した方々の総額資産額は1,000億円を超え、ノウハウと成
功者たちの声（Voice of Success）と呼ばれるように。毎週ボラ
ンティアで成功者インタビューナビライブ視聴回数35万回を
超え多くの人生成功者を輩出。エンターテインメント界にも深
く関わり、ハリウッドセレブやキングオブポップをはじめ世界
的歌手を世に送り出した方々ともプライベートで交流が深く、
グローバルアーティストたちとの時間を「いつも感謝」と「世界
とのつながり」として大切にしている。人生転換期を迎えた人
たちとの出会いにIntuitive Adviso（直観を高めるサポーター）
として、スピリチュアルインスピレーションを贈り続ける。

Love & Light
www.masamilight.com

AMESIAN BOOKS
2535 W. 237th St., Unit 106
Torrance, CA 90505
amesianbooks.com

Copyright © 2020 by AMESIAN BOOKS
All rights reserved.

AMESIAN BOOKS is a division of Wanann, Inc.
No part of this publication may be reproduced,
stored, or transmitted in any form or by any
means, electronic, mechanical, photocopied,
recorded or otherwise, without prior written
consent from the publisher.
Notice of Disclaimer: The information
contained in this book is based on the author's
experience and options. The author and
publisher will not be held liable for the use or
misuse of the information in this book.

Publisher: Kyoichi Ichimura
Art director: Megumi Tamura
Editorial assistant: Risa Akashi

ISBN 978-1-945352-03-4

2 4 6 8 10 9 7 5 3 1

First edition, 2020

WANANN, Inc.

www.ingramcontent.com/pod-product-compliance
Lightning Source LLC
Chambersburg PA
CBHW022008120526
44592CB00034B/736